LOVE

by Jane Belk Moncure
illustrated by Linda Sommers Hohag

THE CHILD'S WORLD

ELGIN, ILLINOIS 60120

Distributed by Childrens Press, 1224 West Van Buren Street, Chicago, Illinois 60607.

Library of Congress Cataloging in Publication Data

Moncure, Jane Belk.
   Love.

   (What is it?)
   SUMMARY: Illustrates ways of demonstrating
love for other people.
   1. Love—Juvenile literature (1. Love)
I. Hohag, Linda. II. Title.
BF575.L8M567 1981   241´.4   80-27479
ISBN 0-89565-205-6

What is love?

When my little brother is sick and can't
play in the snow, and I bring him a pan
of snow, so he can make a snowman—
even a tiny one—that's love.

When we're having a pillow fight, and
he slips off the bed and scrapes his arm,
and I tell him I'm sorry and get him a
bandage, that's love.

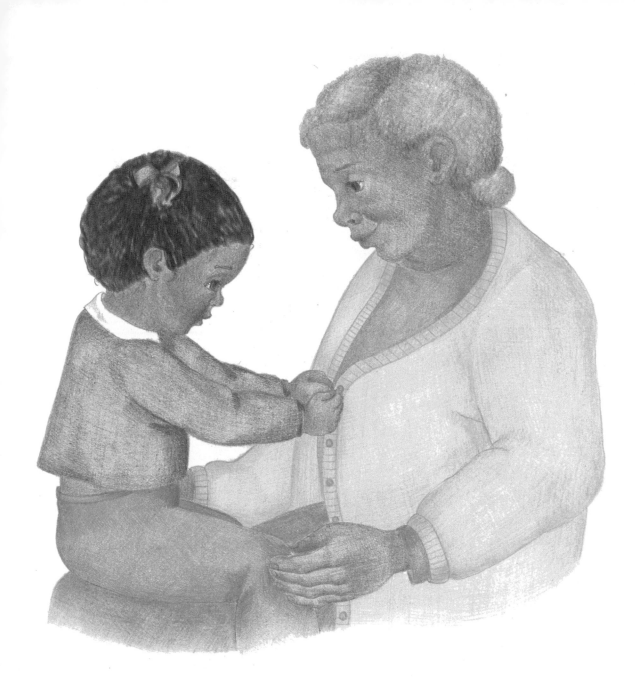

When my Nana is cold and I bring her a sweater and then help her button it so she will be warm, that's love.

Love is helping Mom carry in the groceries and then putting the things away.

When my sister drops her sandwich and
asks for part of mine, and I help her clean
the floor, make her another sandwich—
and give her a napkin—that's love.

When I want to do something, but my parents say, "No," even though I am disappointed, I try to obey. That's love.

Love is taking a cake we just baked to
the new family moving in next door.

When I invite the new neighbor over to
play and show her my secret hiding
place. . .

and on Monday walk with her to school,
that's love.

Cutting a birthday cake so everyone has
a slice, that's love. For love is sharing.

Giving a friend a chance to jump rope
once or twice, that's love. For love is
kindness.

When a friend wants to copy your
paper, love is saying, "No." For
sometimes love is courage.

When you tell Dad that Tommy didn't
break the window, you did, that's love.
For love is honesty.

When Dad tells you to pick up your toys before watching TV, and you cheerfully obey, that's love. For love is obeying.

When my best friend can't have a
birthday party because her Dad is
sick, and I take her a present anyway,
that's love. For love is caring.

Love is treating others as we want
them to treat us.

Sometimes it's a hug and a smile.

The feeling of love is the best of
all feelings.

It comes from caring for others
and knowing others care for us.

Can you think of other ways to
show love?

About the Author:

Jane Belk Moncure, author of many books and stories for young children, is a graduate of Virginia Commonwealth University and Columbia University. She has taught nursery, kindergarten and primary children in Europe and America. Mrs. Moncure has taught early childhood education while serving on the faculties of Virginia Commonwealth University and the University of Richmond. She was the first president of the Virginia Association for Early Childhood Education and has been recognized widely for her services to young children. She is married to Dr. James A. Moncure, Vice President of Elon College, and currently lives in Burlington, North Carolina.

About the Artist:

Linda Hohag is a graduate of the Cleveland Institute of Art in Cleveland, Ohio. She worked for the American Greeting Corporation in Cleveland, Ohio, for several years; and for the past seven years she has worked as a freelance artist. In addition to illustrating many, many books for children, Mrs. Hohag has designed products for the Toystalgia Company and the Stancraft Corporation. Mrs. Hohag says her favorite kind of work is illustrating children's books.